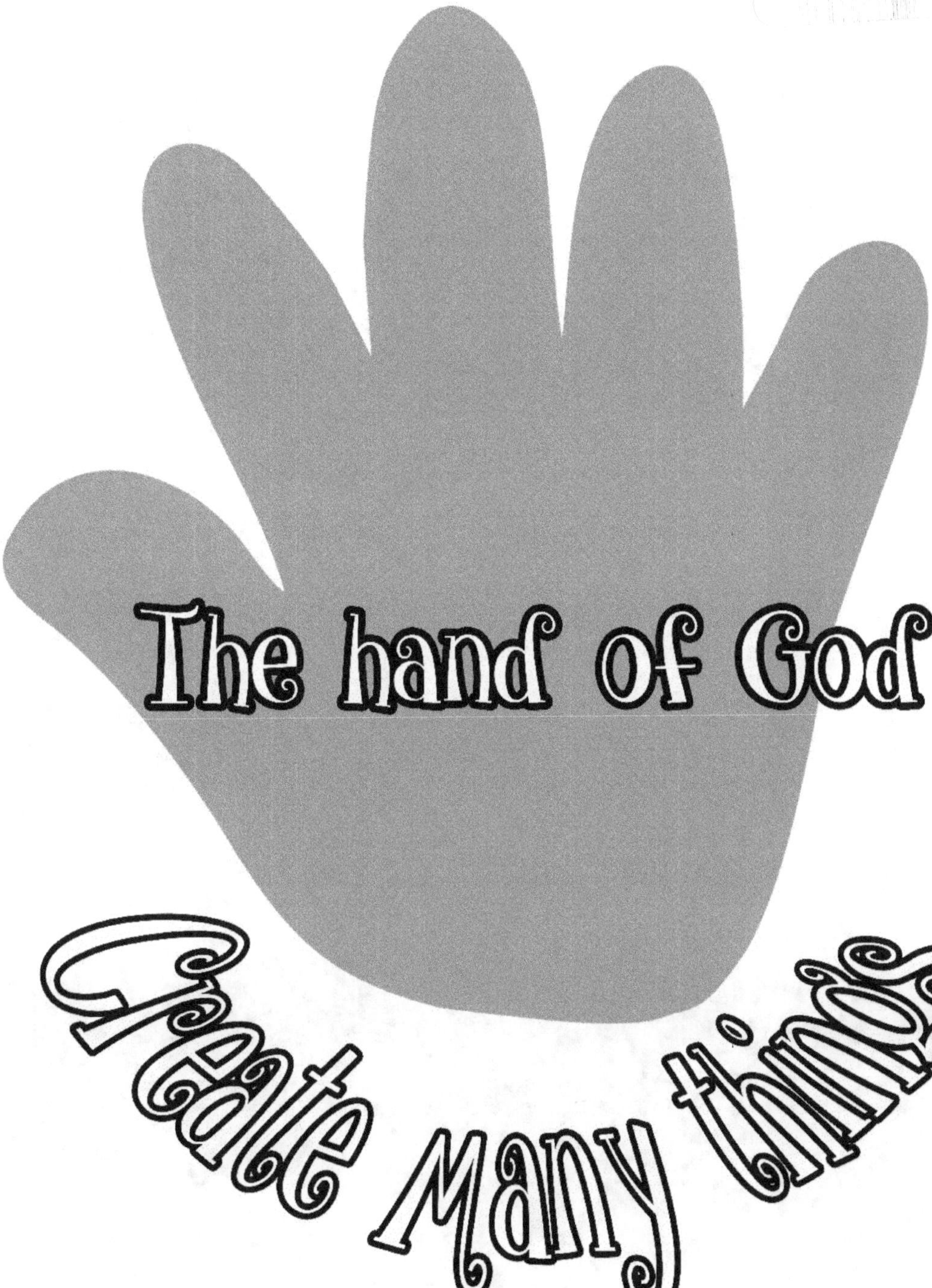

The hand of God

Create many things.

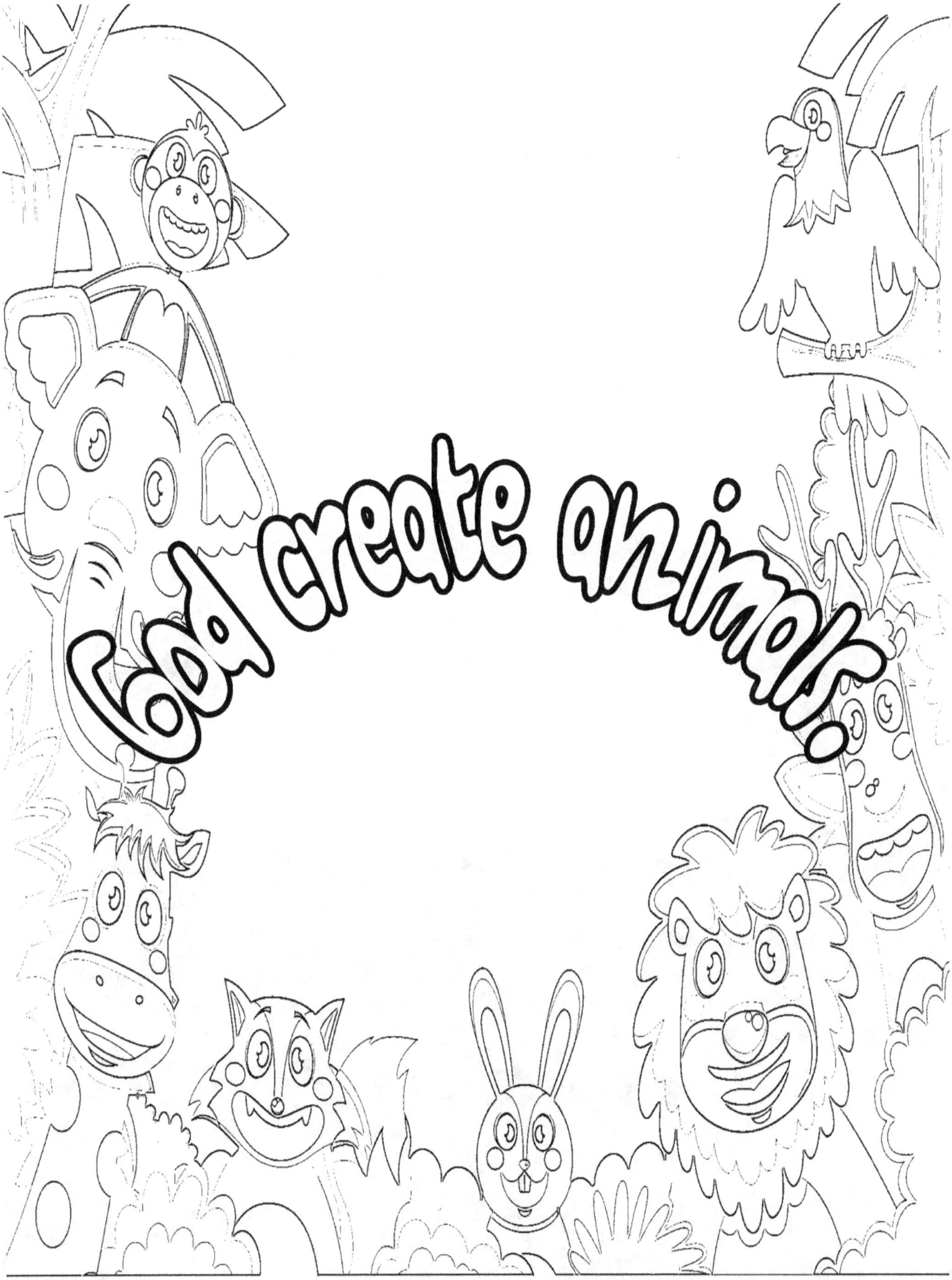
God create animals.

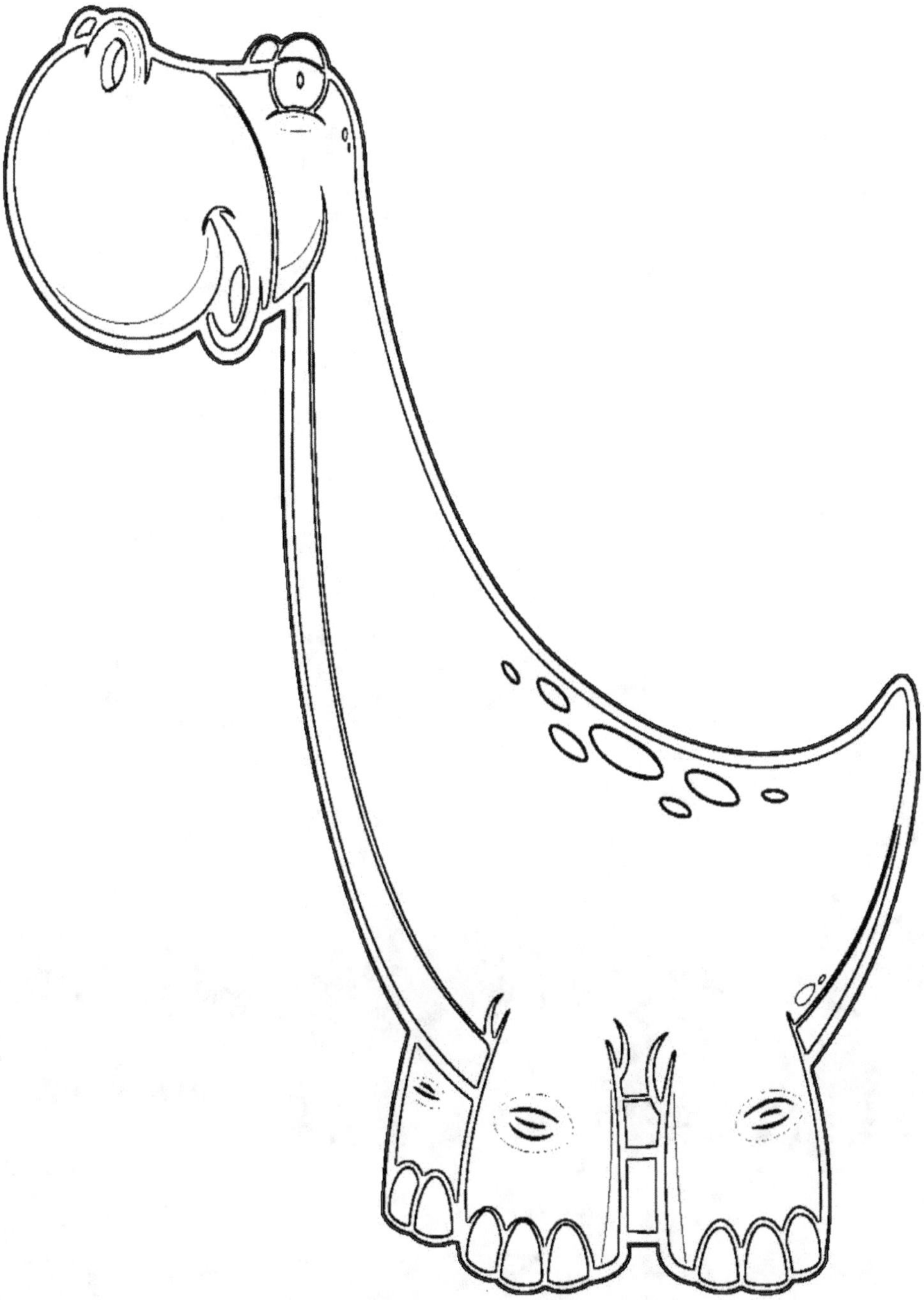

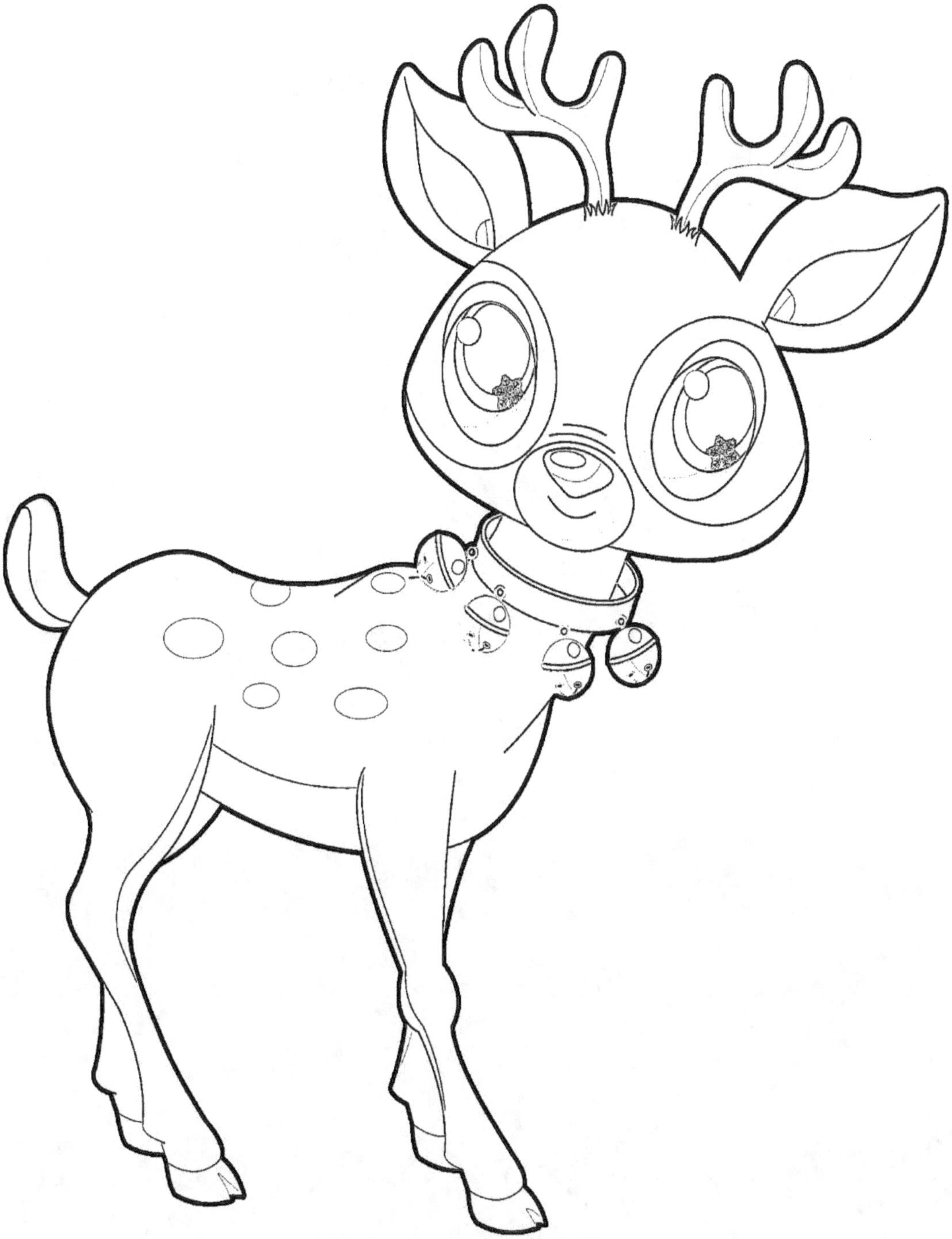

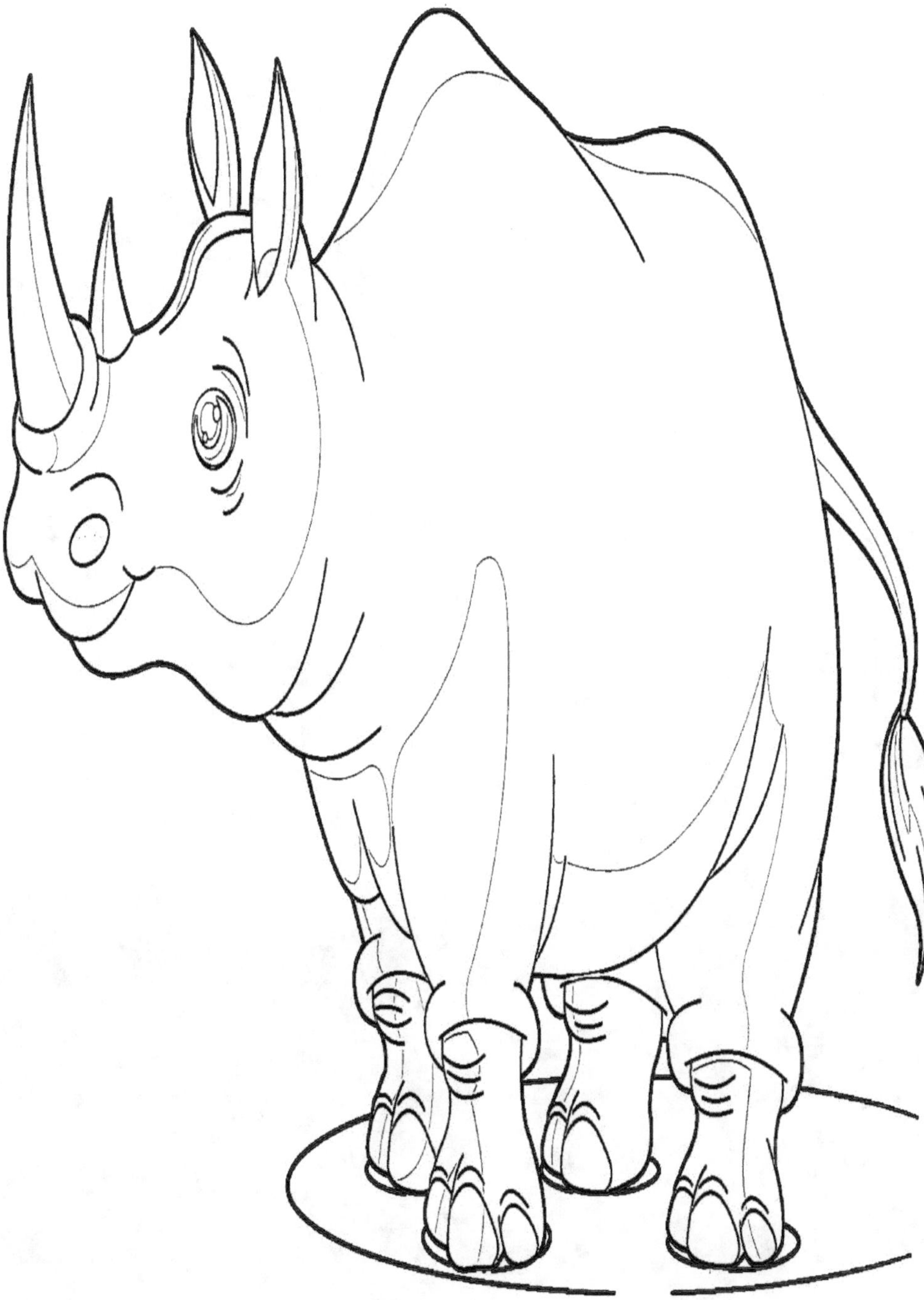

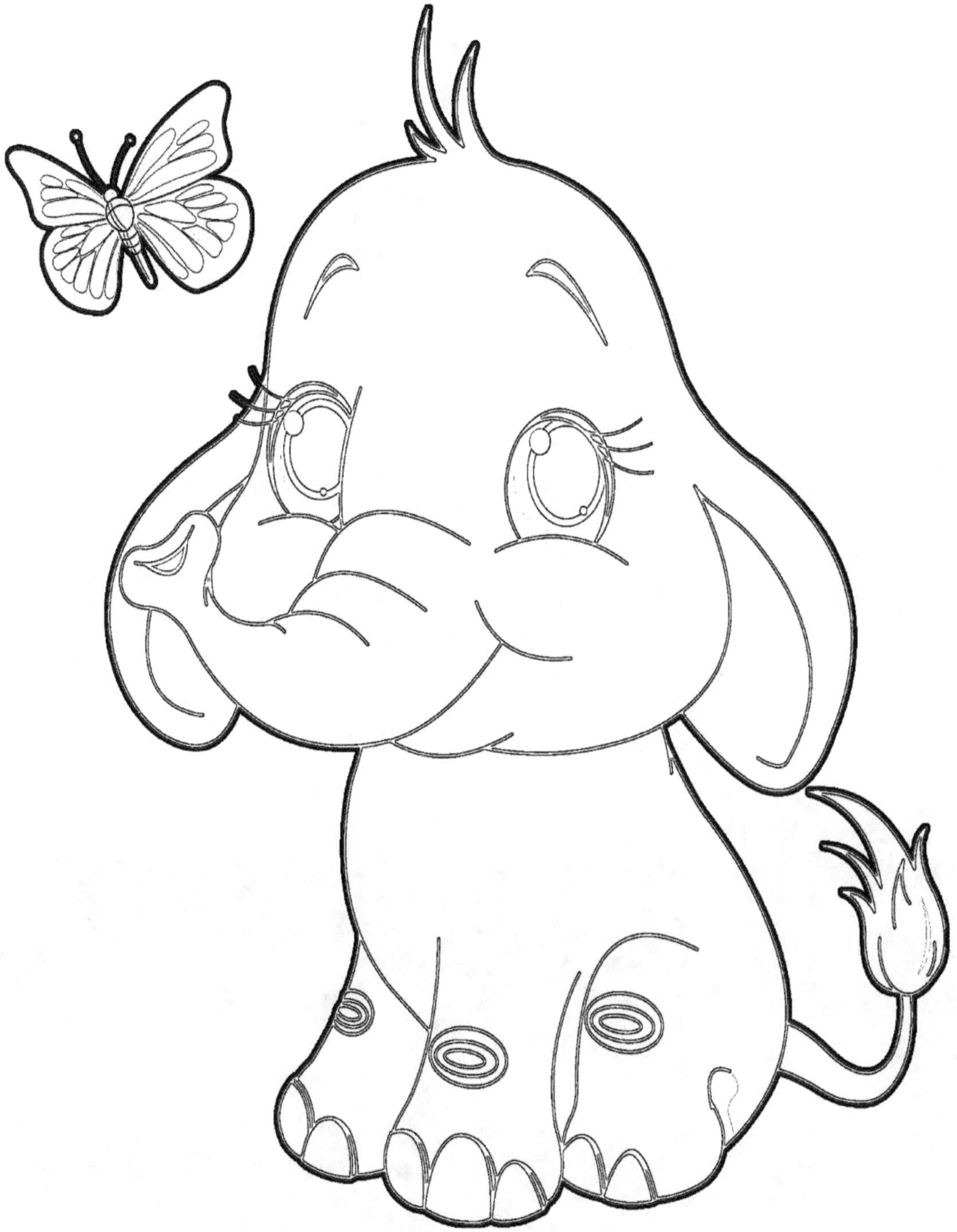

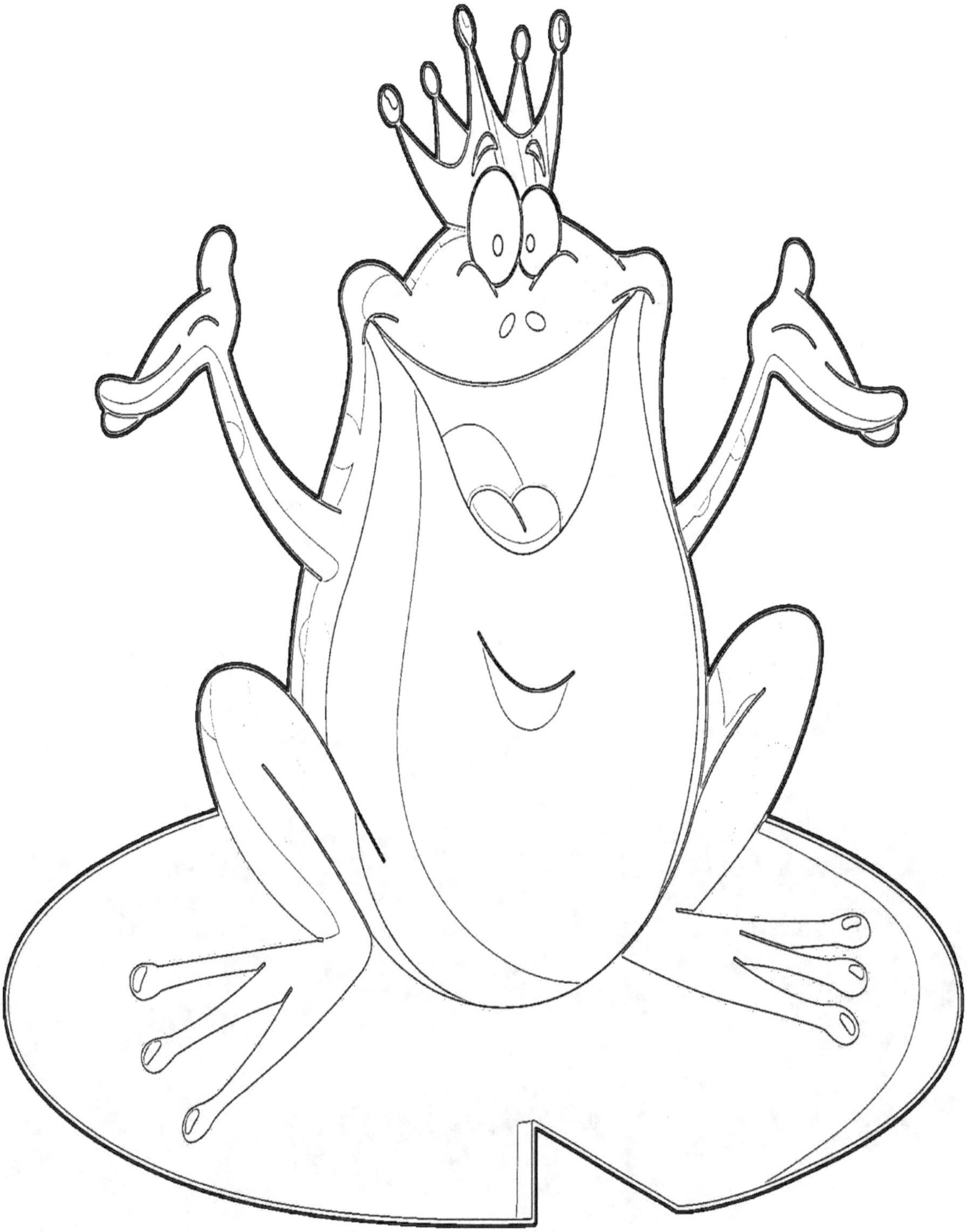

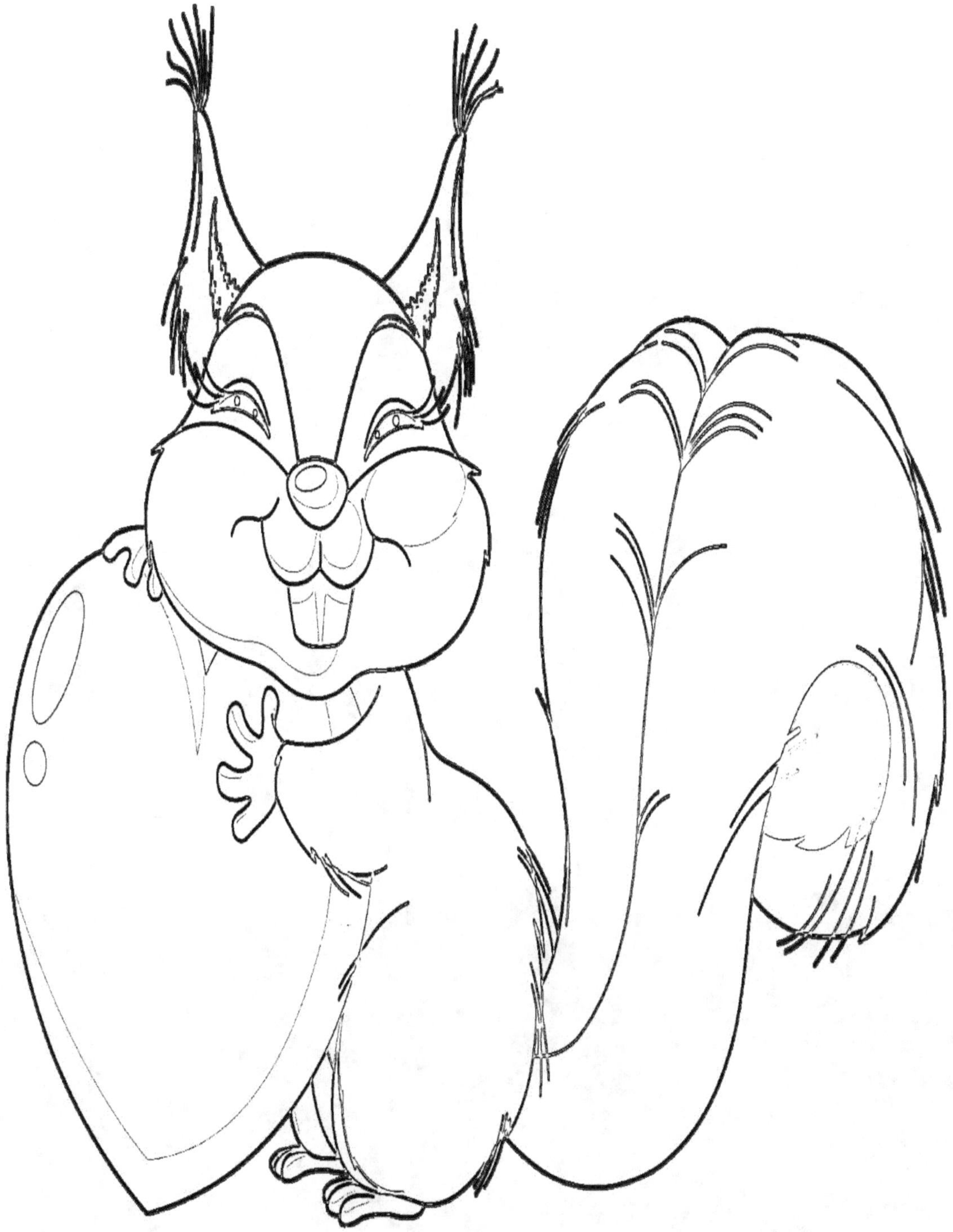

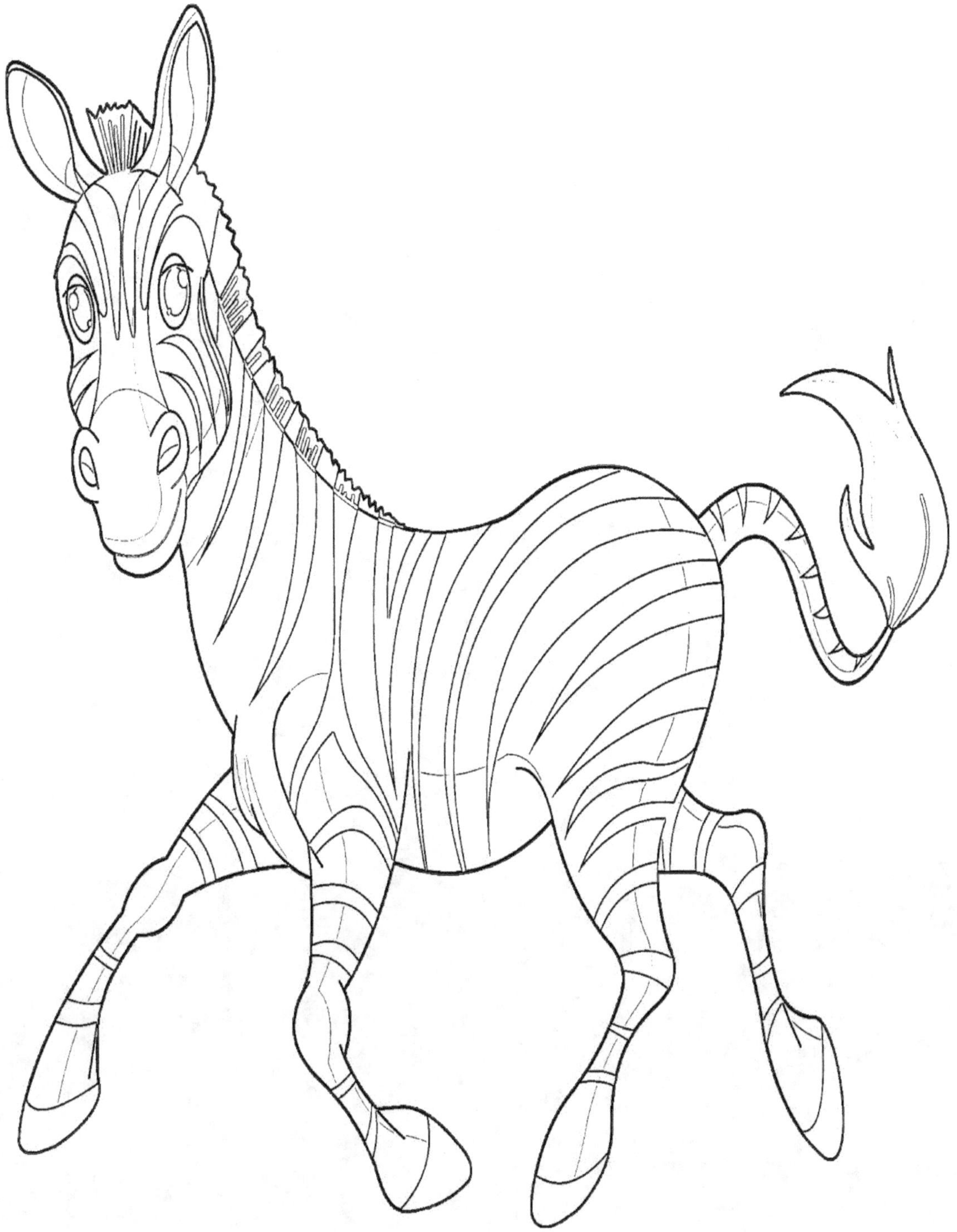

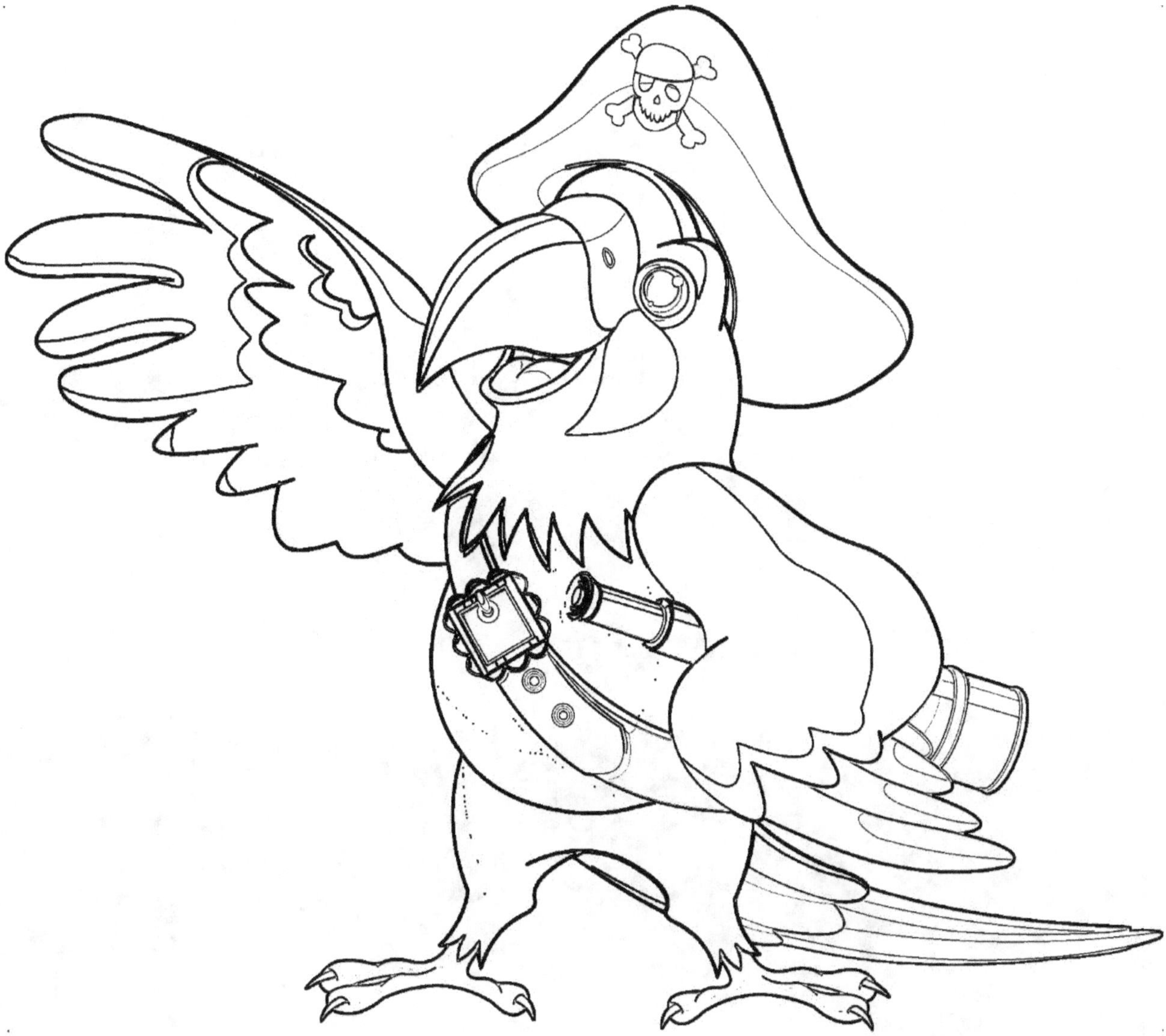

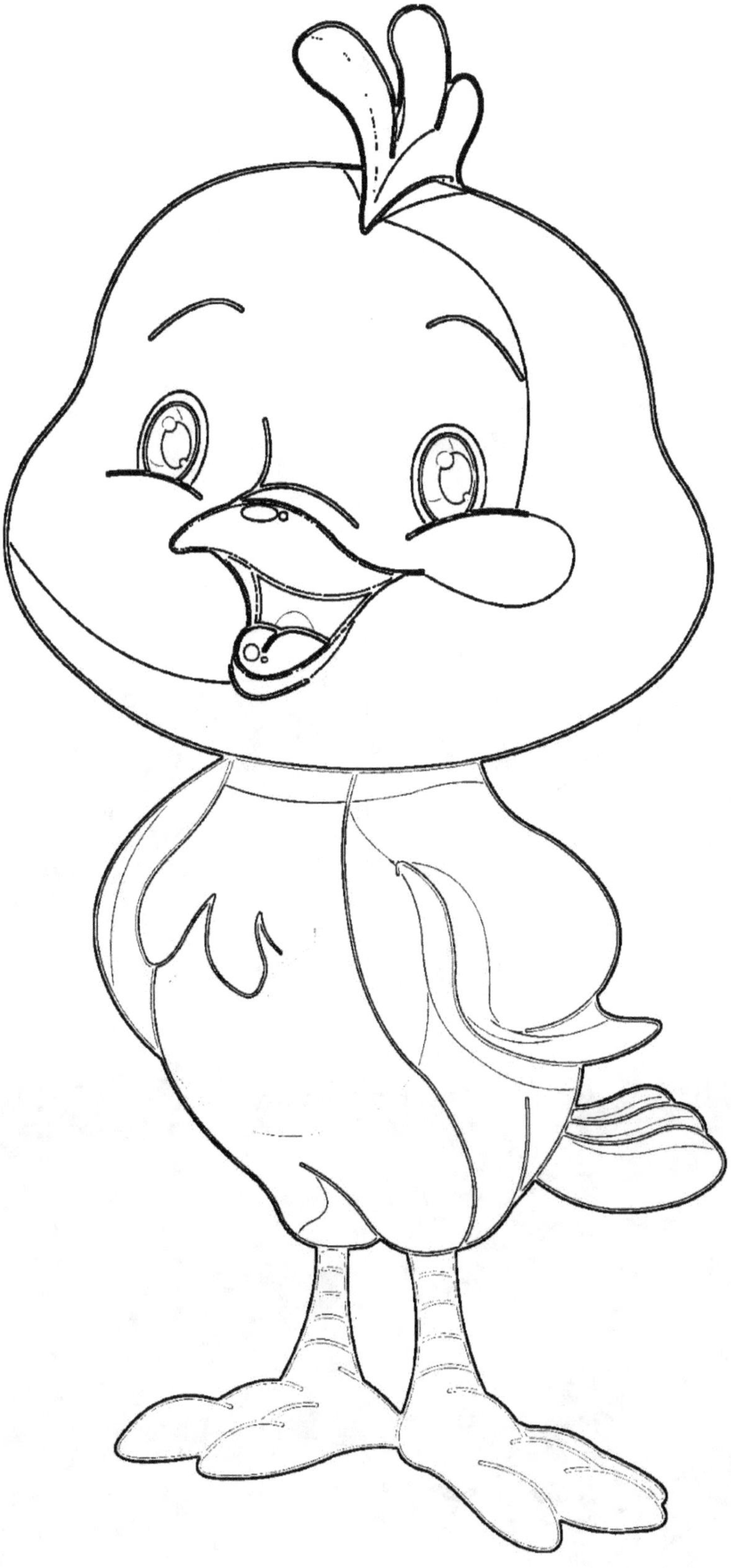

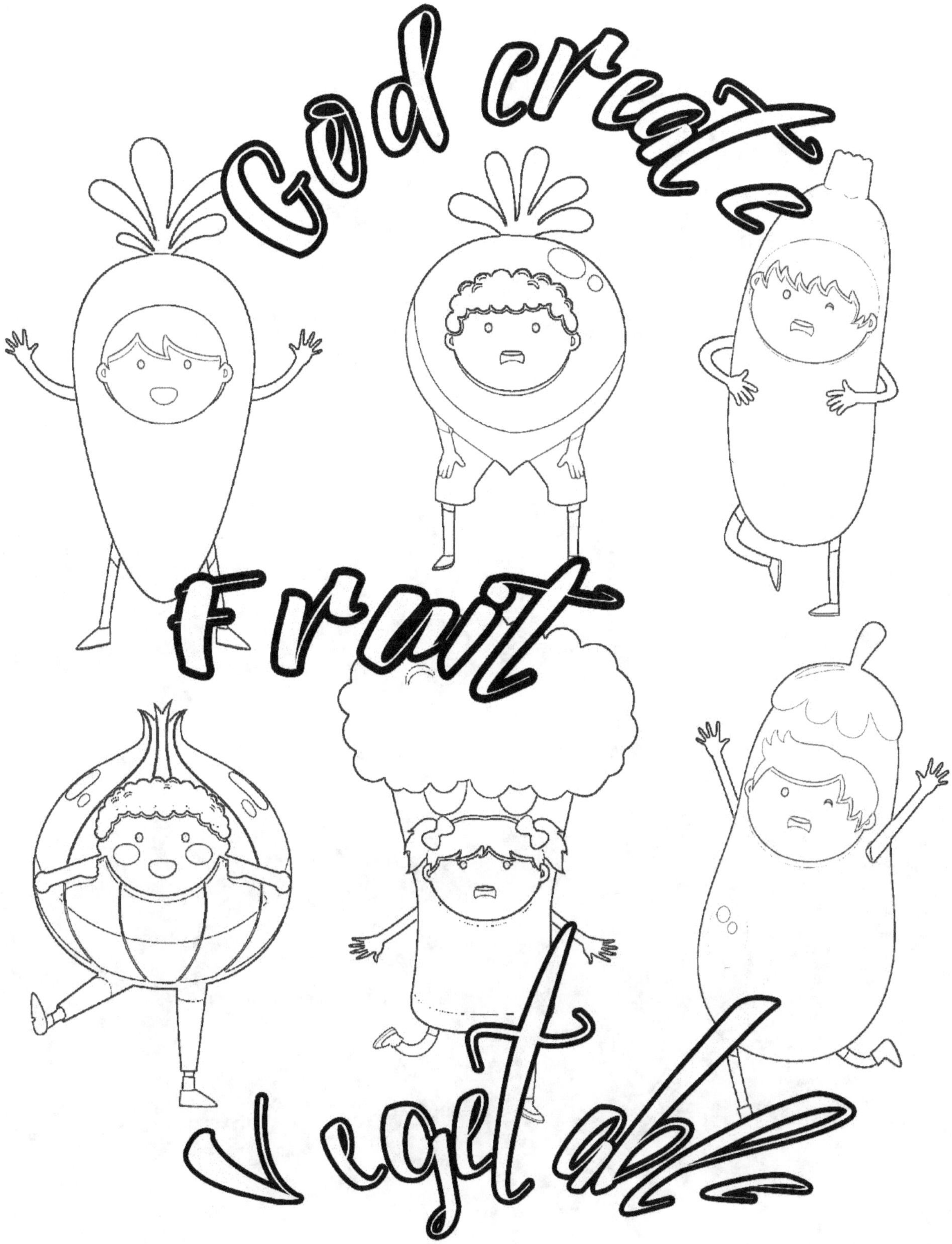
God create
Fruit
Vegetable

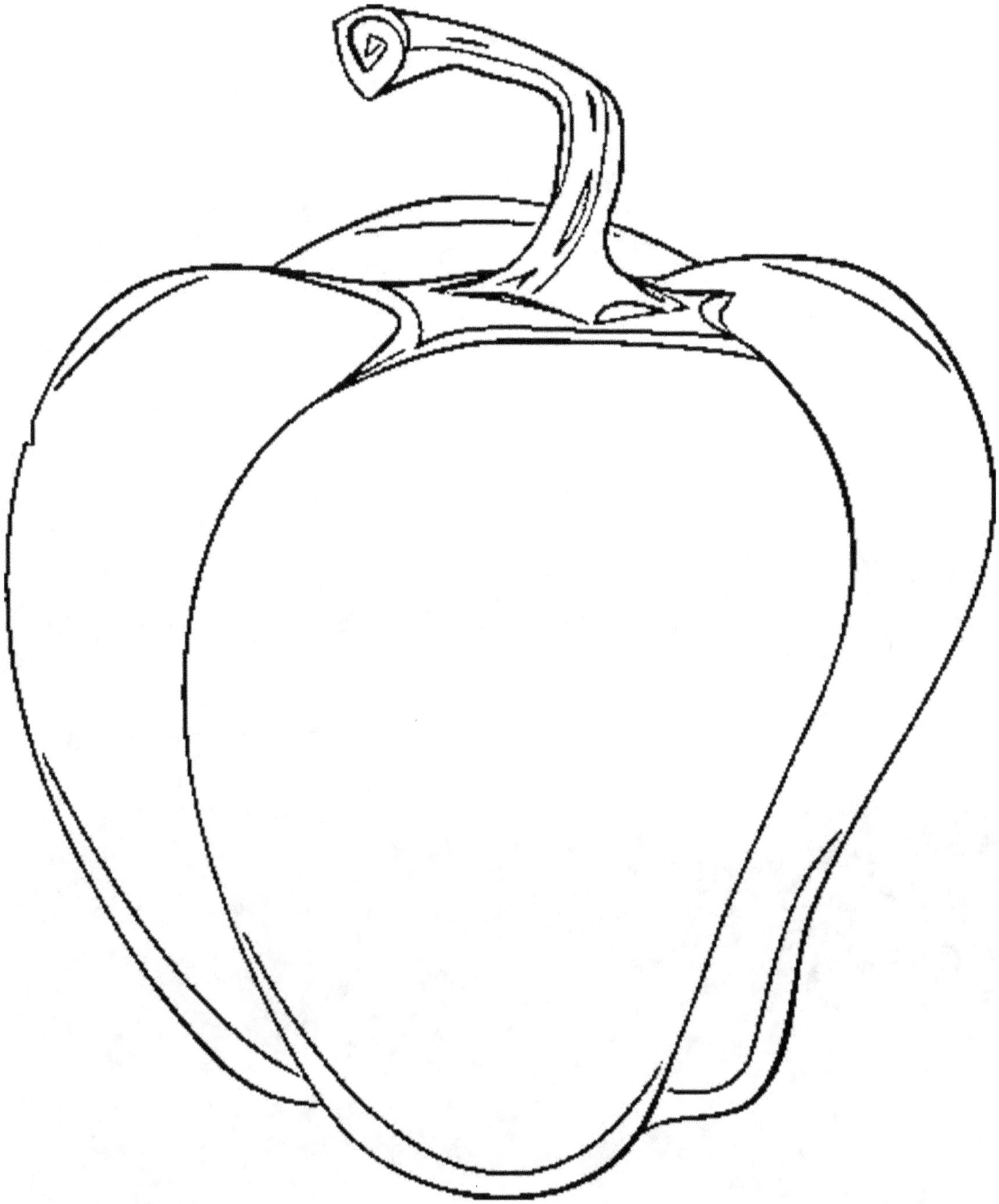

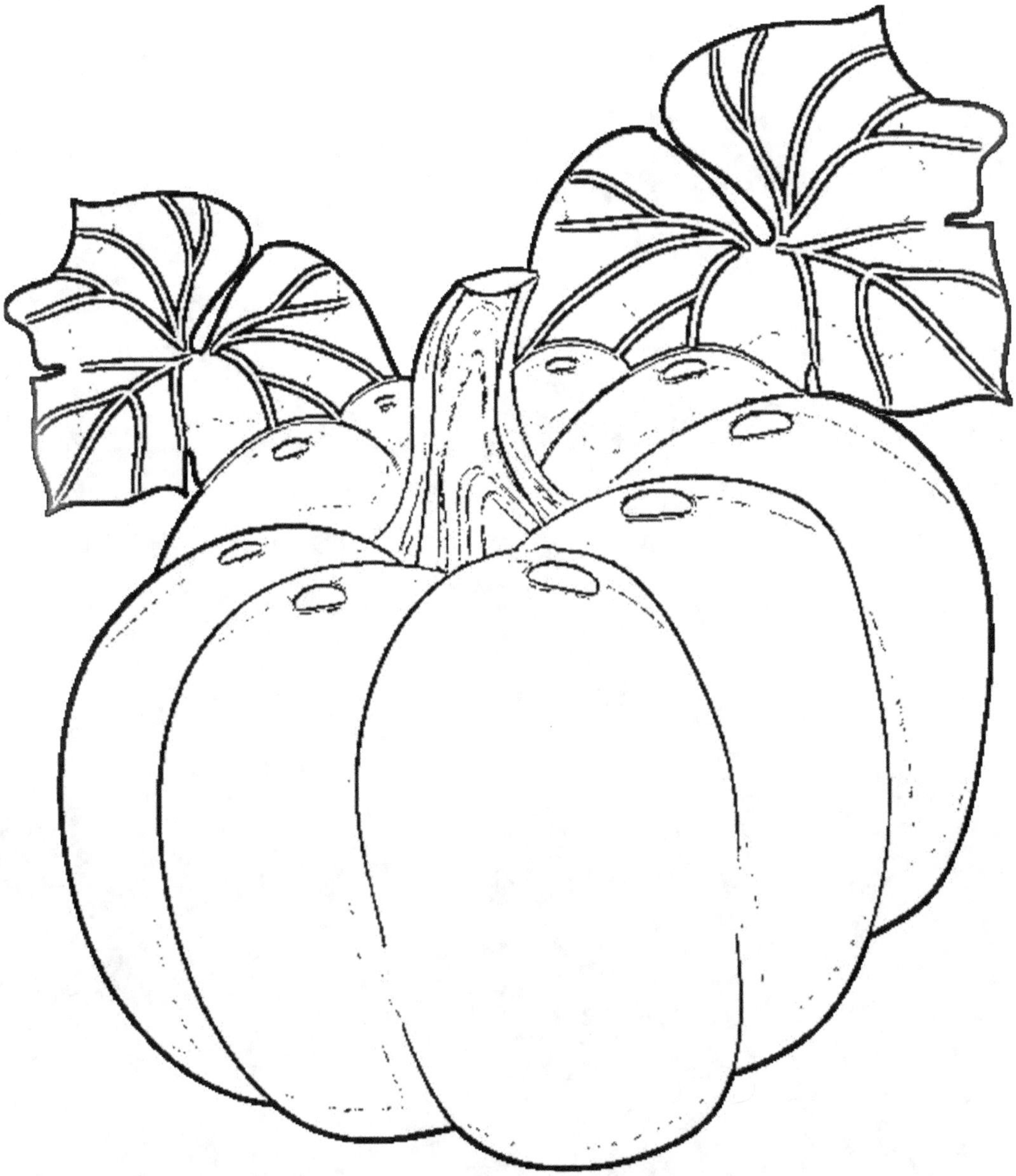

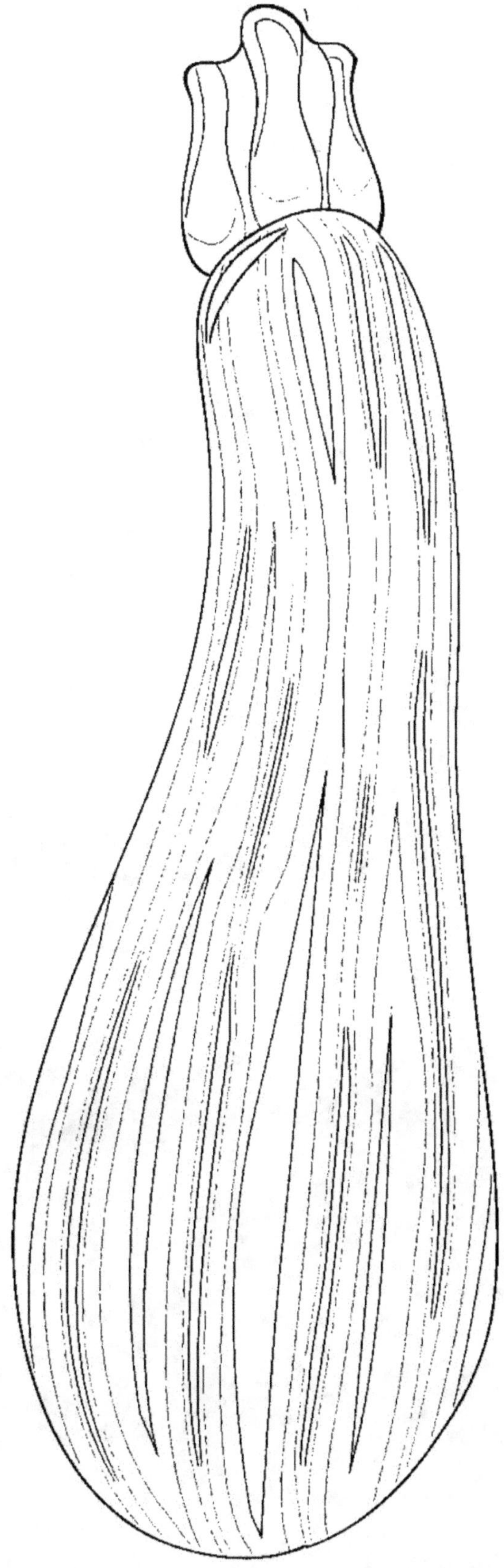

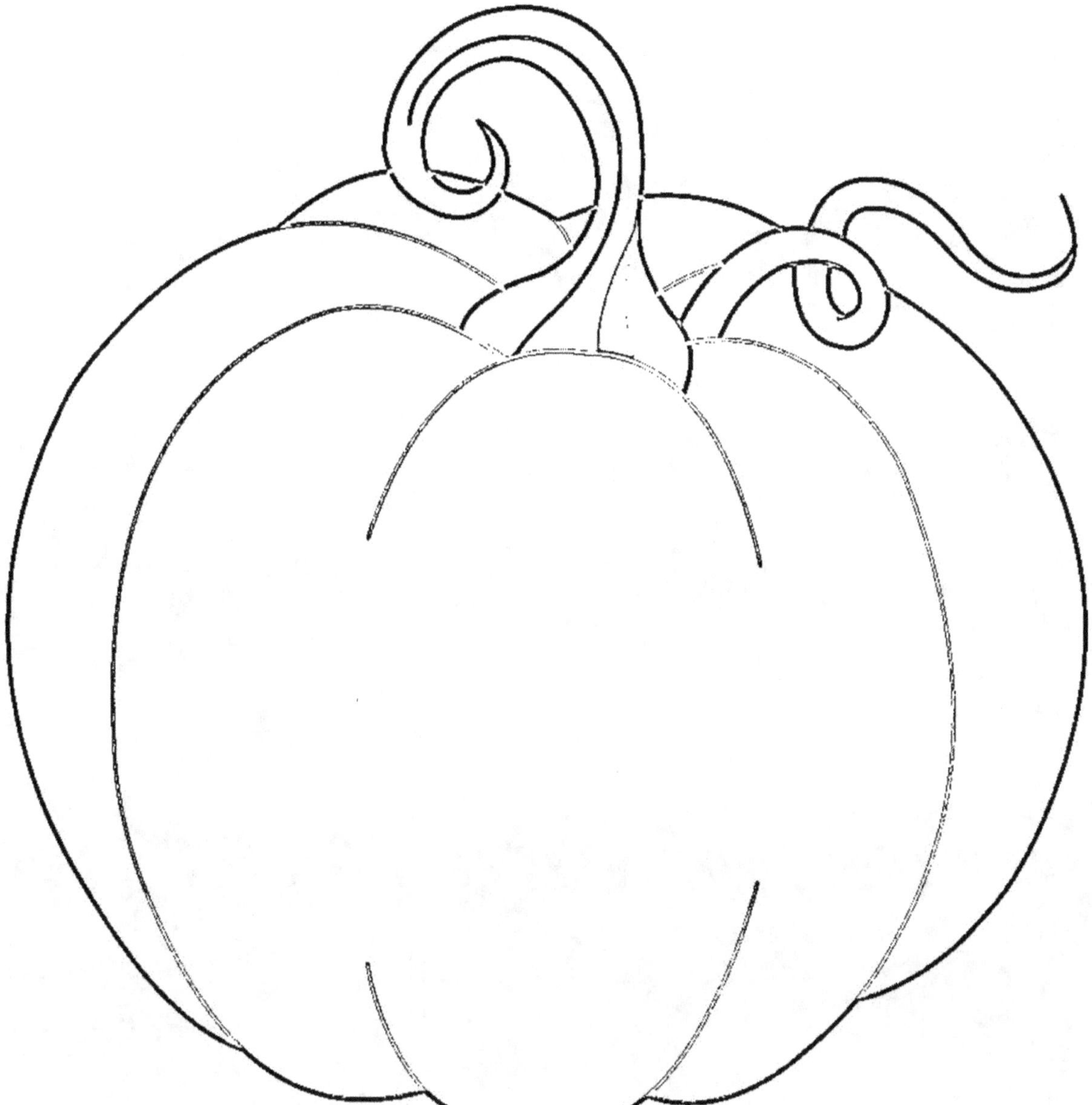

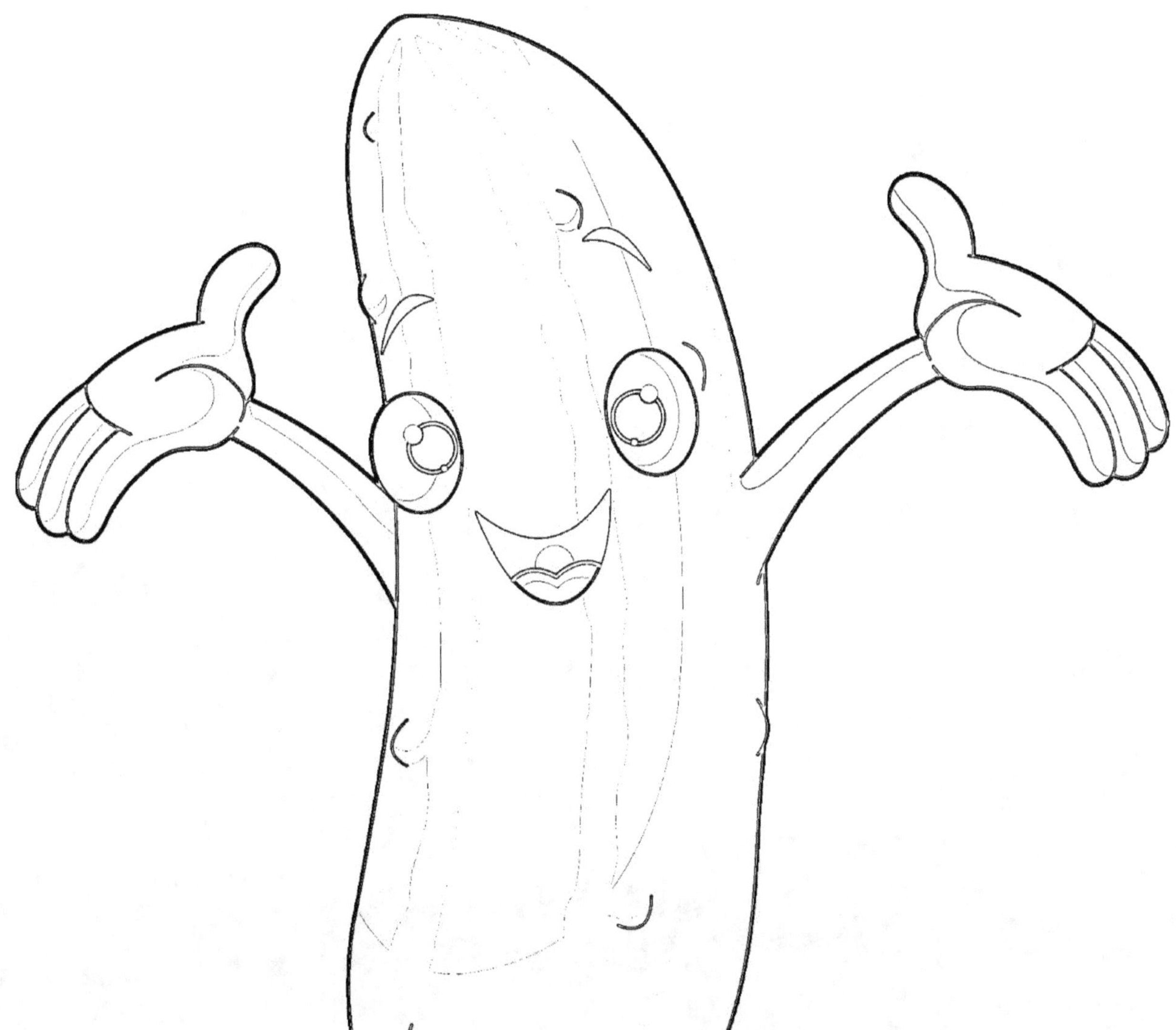

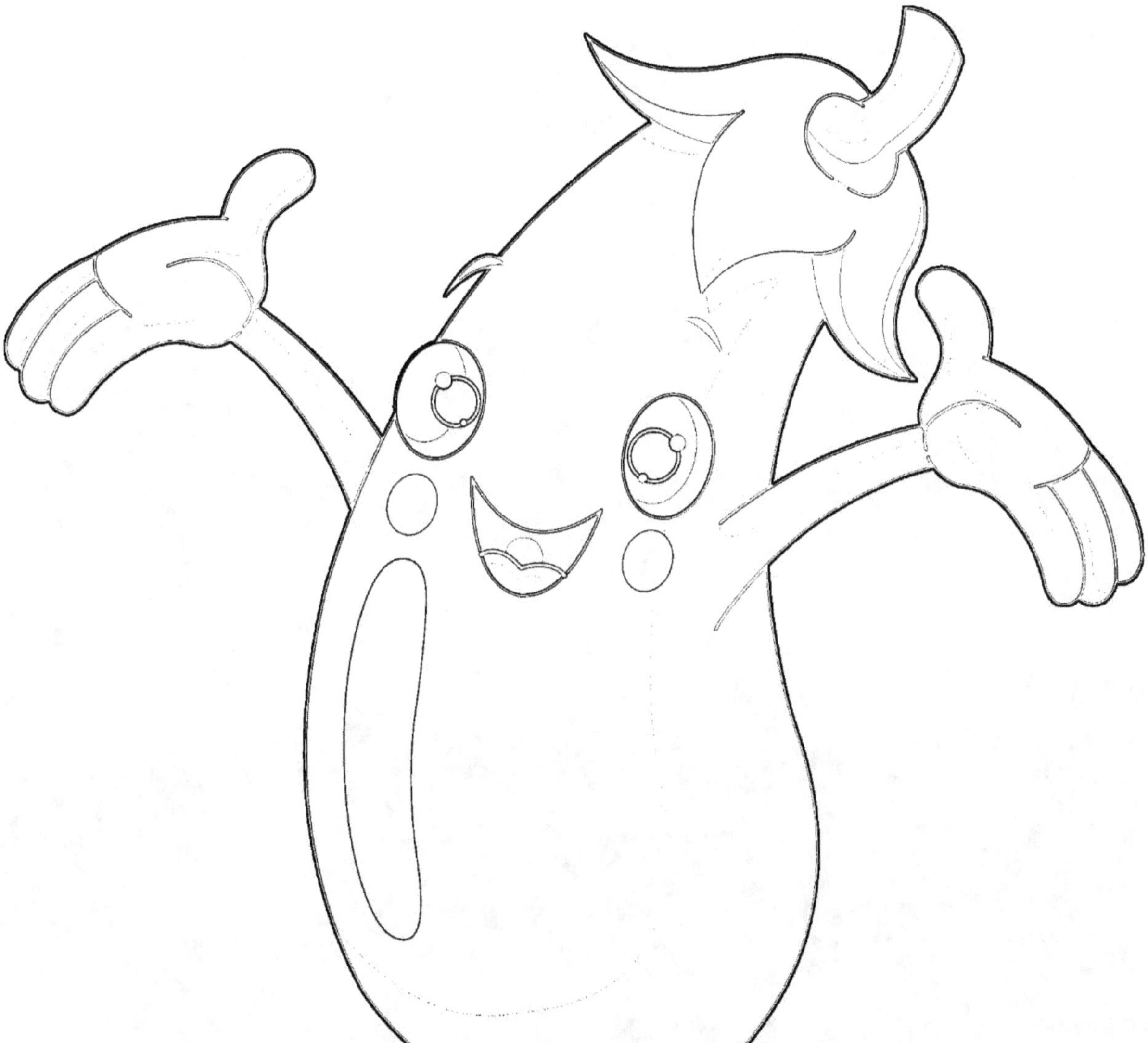

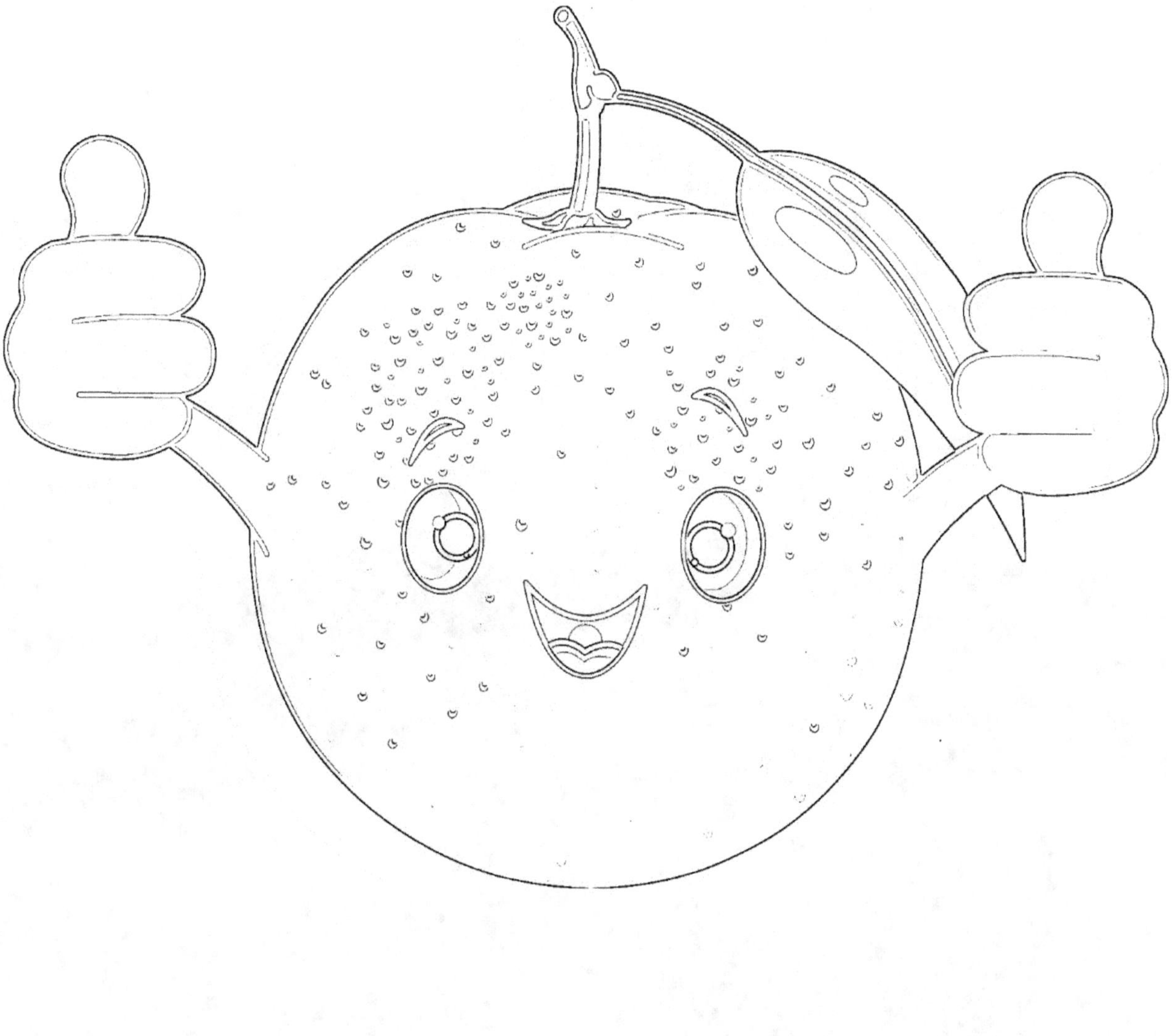

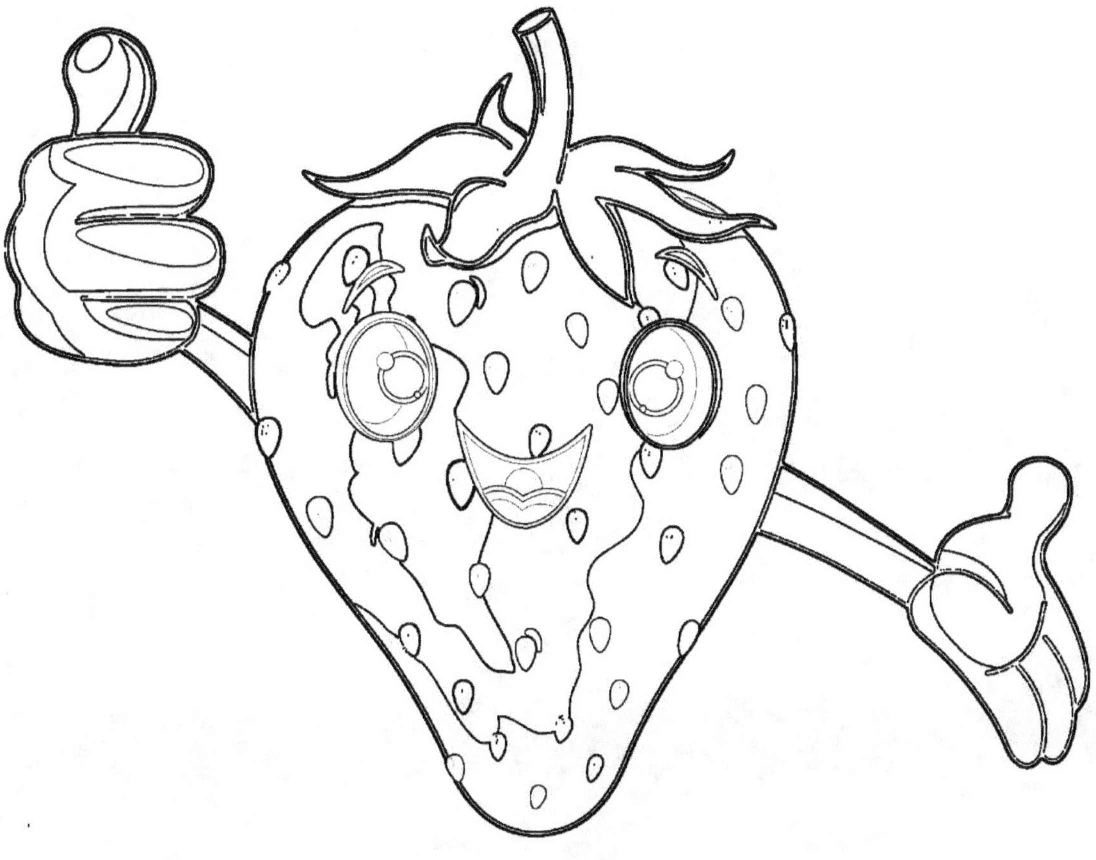

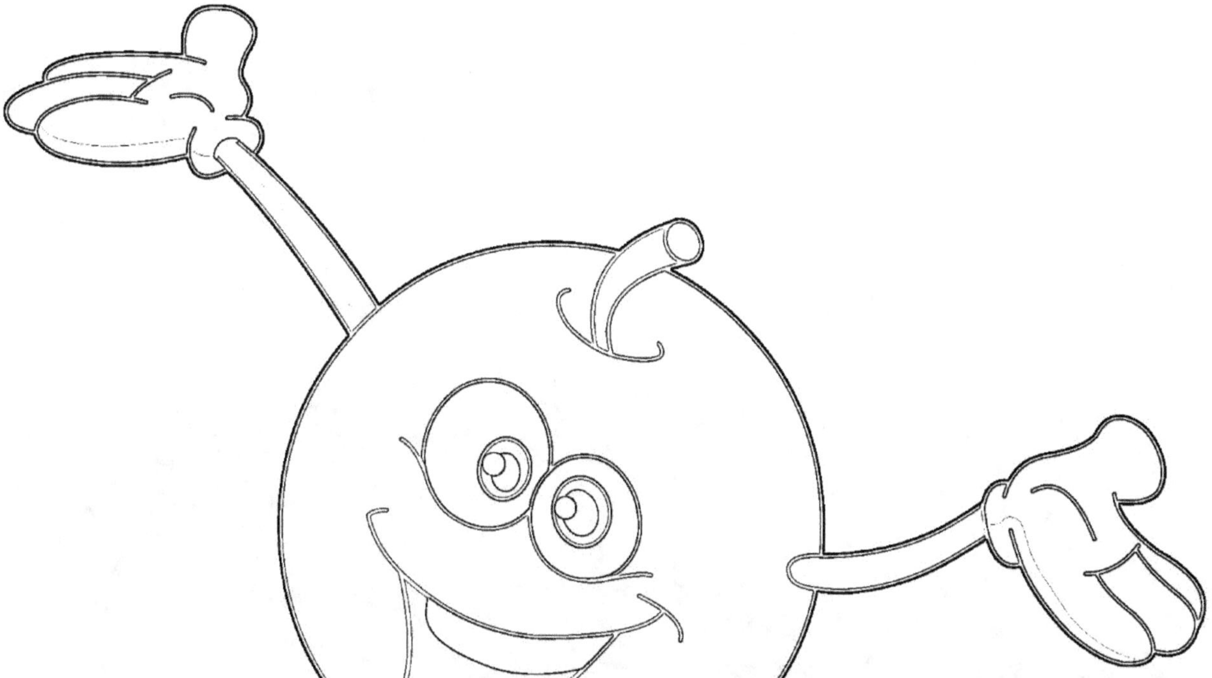

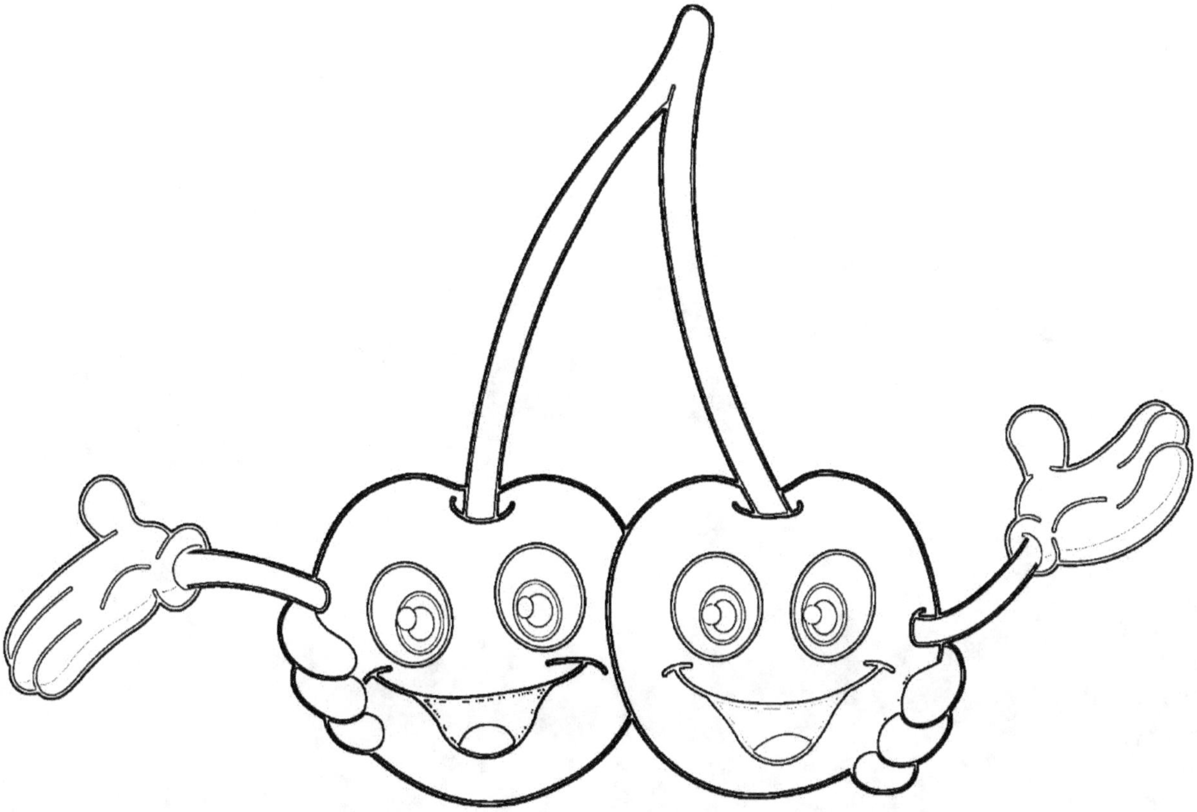

GOD CREATE ALL THINGS

GOD

OUR CREATOR

www.ingramcontent.com/pod-product-compliance
Lightning Source LLC
Chambersburg PA
CBHW081753170526
45167CB00009B/4018